BORN to Be GIANTS

Born to Be Giants

How Baby Dinosaurs Grew to Rule the World

Lita Judge

Rb,
*Flash
Point*

ROARING BROOK PRESS
NEW YORK

DINOSAURS!

The word makes us think of ferocious,

blood-thirsty, **KILLER GIANTS.**

It also makes us think of

TRAIN-LONG,

SKYSCRAPER-TALL

GARGANTUANS!

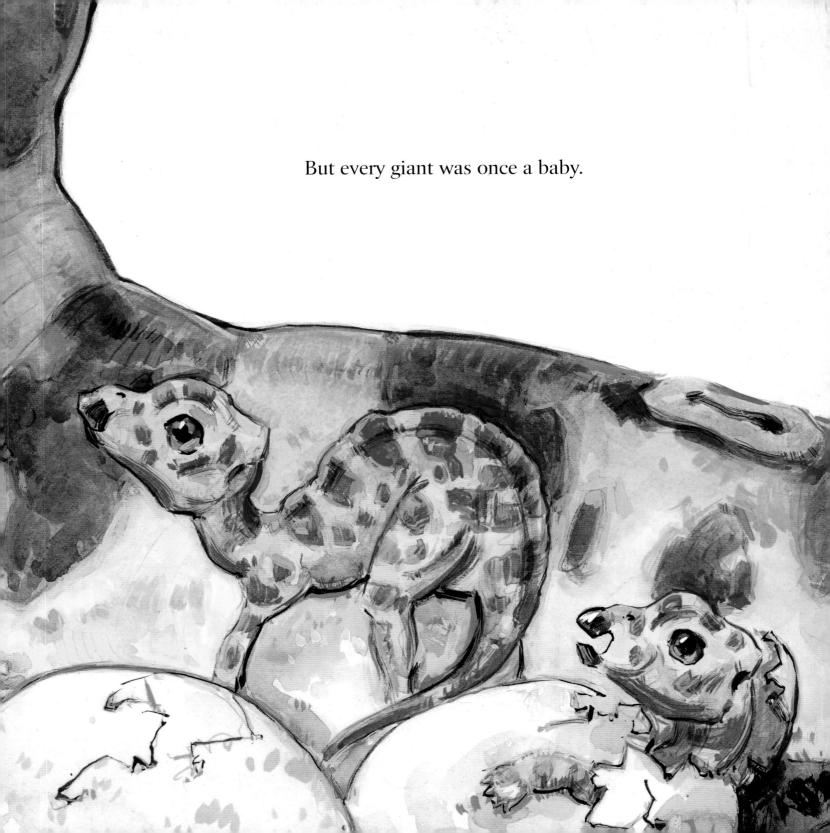

But every giant was once a baby.

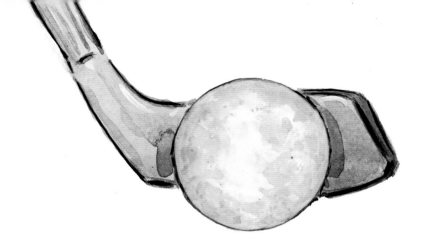

Baby **DINOSAURS** hatched from eggs.
Some eggs were as small as a golf ball.

The largest were as big
as a loaf of French bread.

Paleontologists (scientists who study the remains of prehistoric plants and animals) search for clues about baby dinosaurs by looking for their fossils.

In South America, a site was found where thousands of grapefruit-sized fossilized eggs were so closely packed together that it was hard to walk without stepping on one. Inside some of the eggs were dinosaur embryos with long necks and tails, peg-shaped teeth, and armored skin. They were a type of titanosaur, probably **SALTASAURUS**.

A herd of *Saltasaurus* mothers must have gathered by the riverbank to bury their eggs in the sand. In a few days, these giant, plant-eating mothers would have stripped the forest bare and moved on in search of more food. Weeks later, the eggs hatched and the sand slithered with babies, each smaller than the footprints their mothers left behind.

The largest dinosaurs probably didn't raise their babies. A mother **ARGENTINOSAURUS** might have weighed as much as 17 elephants. But the largest dinosaur eggs found are only 18 inches long.

That means a newly-hatched *Argentinosaurus* barely reached its mother's toes. These mothers probably couldn't protect their tiny babies without trampling them underfoot.

A herd of *Argentinosaurus* was an earth-shaking, bone-crushing stampede of feet. Their tiny babies probably hid under forest cover. Hungry, meat-eating dinosaurs stalked them for a bite-sized meal. Huge crocodiles ate them. Even little mammals ate them. The babies were hungry all the time and had to find their next meal without becoming one! Only a few survived.

Some mother dinosaurs may have protected their nests even though they couldn't sit on their eggs to incubate them. **TYRANNOSAURUS REX** mothers were too heavy to sit on their nests, but recent fossil discoveries show that babies of another dinosaur in the tyrannosaurid family stayed with their parents after hatching.

Mothers may have built mound nests similar to those made by bush turkeys today. Bush turkeys build mound nests from leaves and sand. Like a compost heap, the leaves produce heat as they rot, keeping the eggs warm.

We can learn a lot about dinosaurs by studying living animals. Today, crocodiles look almost as fierce as *Tyrannosaurus rex*, but they are protective mothers and guard their mound nests and their hatchlings. It's not hard to imagine how a *Tyrannosaurus rex* may have protected her nest.

A bad-tempered *Tyrannosaurus rex* mother probably ate anyone who tried stealing her eggs. She stood guard over her warm, smelly mound nest. Leftovers from her last meal rotted nearby. Insects swarmed the rotting meat and piles of dinosaur poop.

Fossils now show that at least some dinosaurs brooded their eggs like birds. In 1923, a new species of dinosaur was found lying on top of a nest. At first scientists thought the dinosaur had died while raiding the nest—it had a huge, toothless beak that looked perfect for eating eggs. They named it **OVIRAPTOR**, which means "Egg Thief." But 70 years later, paleontologists found more of these dinosaurs on top of nests. By looking at the embryos inside the eggs, they discovered that these were *Oviraptor* parents sitting on their own nests.

SINOSAUROPTERYX
a feathered dinosaur

DILONG
a feathered tyrannosaur

Not only were these dinosaurs sitting on nests like birds, they may have looked like birds as well. Several new species of feathered dinosaurs have recently been found. These new discoveries have completely changed how we think dinosaurs looked. They've convinced most paleontologists that not all dinosaurs went extinct. Some may have evolved to become today's birds.

OVIRAPTOR
perhaps had feathers

CAUDIPTERYX
feathered, close relative to Oviraptor

TROODON
perhaps had feathers

PROTARCHAEOPTERYX
a feathered but flightless dinosaur

ARCHAEOPTERYX
the first bird

HARRIS'S HAWK
a living bird

TYRANNOSAURUS REX
closely related to Dilong, perhaps fosilized feathers will be found

MICRORAPTOR
four winged, feathered

SINORNITHOSAURUS
feathered dinosaur

EOALULAVIS
early bird

Though he couldn't fly, a father *Oviraptor* might have spread his feathers over his fragile babies to keep them cool in the searing desert sun while mother brought meat for their next meal. He may also have used his feathers to keep his babies warm at night.

Some plant-eating dinosaurs kept their nests safe by grouping into large colonies. Over a thousand fossilized nests of **HYPACROSAURUS**, a duck-billed dinosaur, were found in one area!

Penguins, pelicans, and many seabirds gather at huge nesting sites today. The nests are clustered with just enough space to fit babies and adults. The parents work together, alerting each other if a predator comes near.

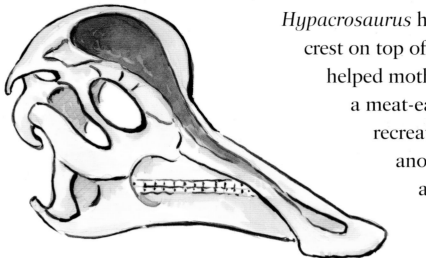

Hypacrosaurus had a hollow, bony nasal crest on top of its head. Perhaps the crest helped mothers warn each other when a meat-eater stalked near. Scientists recreated the hollow crest of another duck-billed dinosaur and found that it made a sound like a trombone.

Could a herd of mother dinosaurs have blasted out a brass-band alert call?

Imagine thousands of *Hypacrosaurus* mothers and tens of thousands of babies stretched as far as the eye can see. A pack of swift, cunning *Troodon* prowled the edge of the nesting colony, waiting to unleash a lightning fast raid on unprotected babies. Suddenly an alarm sounded. *Hooooonk!* More mothers shrieked. Angry and fierce, they mobbed the attackers. The *Troodon* pack slunk away, hungry.

Dinosaur parents might have worked together in other ways, such as babysitting. Modern ostriches take turns guarding babies in a group called a crèche while other adults forage for food.

A fossilized **PSITTACOSAURUS** was found with 34 babies clustered around it. We don't know how many eggs this small dinosaur laid, but 34 is very likely too many.

Perhaps the *Psittacosaurus* was looking after another mother's babies as well as her own.

A fossilized *Repenomamus*, a mammal about the size of a fox, was found with baby *Psittacosaurus* in its ribcage! We don't usually think of mammals eating dinosaurs—during the time of dinosaurs, most mammals were mouse- or rat-sized—but *Repenomamus* was large enough to hunt small dinosaurs.

Perhaps a fierce *Repenomamus*
caught the scent of his next meal at
the mouth of a burrow. He looked
like a huge Tasmanian Devil and he
was just as fierce. Inside, dozens of
baby *Psittacosaurus* huddled under
a babysitting mother. If he caught
them, he'd swallow them whole. With
predators on the prowl, *Psittacosaurus*
parents couldn't leave their babies
unguarded for a moment.

Some baby dinosaurs may have needed to be fed by their parents! A dinosaur nesting site discovered at Egg Mountain, in western Montana, gave us the first clues of this behavior. A few of the nests contained eggs. Other nests contained newly hatched babies, while still others had older, larger babies. This showed that the babies had stayed in their nests to grow after hatching. Even though they were too heavy to sit on the nests, the mothers probably stayed close by to feed their young. These dinosaurs were given the name **MAIASAURA**, which means "Good Mother Lizard."

Most bird species today are altricial. Their babies are helpless when they hatch, with wobbly, undeveloped legs and weak necks. The hatchlings must stay in the nest until they grow stronger and older. It is likely that *Maiasaura* were altricial—like robins today.

Some bird species are precocial. Their babies hatch with developed leg bones and can leave the nest after hatching. These babies often stay with their parents for protection, but get food for themselves. Dinosaurs such as *Saltasaurus* were probably precocial—like geese today.

Baby *Maiasaura* could easily
be trampled by a mother who
weighed as much as four pick-
up trucks. Their mud nest was
a good place to stay out of the
way. Hatchlings teetered and
wobbled like baby birds and
stretched tiny faces up toward
their mother's enormous head.
Imagine the noise all those
baby dinosaurs made as they
squawked hungrily for food!

Predators like **TROODON** might have learned hunting skills growing up in nesting colonies. Paleontologists believe many small, meat-eating dinosaurs lived in packs and hunted prey much larger than themselves.

Today, predators like wolves hunt in packs. Through playful roughhousing, wolf pups strengthen muscles and learn to hunt together.

Fossilized *Troodon* nests were discovered with adult and baby fossils together. They also contained bones of plant-eating dinosaurs, a clue that parents probably brought meat back to their babies.

Perhaps *Troodon* youngsters chased and played tug-of-war with meat their parents brought. They were too young to leave the safety of their island nesting ground. Play helped them grow strong and swift. Soon they'd be cunning hunters and work together as a pack.

Many dinosaurs found safety against such fierce pack-hunters by living together in herds. These herds walked through soft mud, which later hardened into rock, leaving hundreds of fossilized footprints, called trackways.

Today, animals like caribou eat and travel in herds for protection against predators. Packs of wolves stalk the herd, looking for old, small, or young animals because they are weaker and easier prey. The herd works together to alert each other when a predator comes near.

Argentinosaurus belonged to a group of dinosaurs known as sauropods, huge plant-eaters with long necks and tails, and small heads. Sauropod trackways show the footprints of adults and half-grown youngsters, but never babies.

Fossil remains of half-grown sauropods—but again, never small babies—have also been found with adults in bonebeds. Tiny babies probably hatched on their own and didn't join the herd until they were about half grown—large enough to avoid being trampled by the others.

A young *Argentinosaurus* has grown large enough to join a herd. As a baby, he found protection from hungry meat-eaters by hiding in the forest. Soon he'll be big enough to eat from the tops of trees. He'll become one of the **BIGGEST** creatures to ever walk the land, **SHAKING** the ground with each step. Tiny babies did grow into **GIANTS**—in the time of the

DINOSAURS!

More About the Dinosaurs in this Book

TRIASSIC PERIOD	JURASSIC PERIOD	CRETACEOUS PERIOD

245 million
years ago

205 million
years ago

144 million
years ago

65 million
years ago

ARGENTINOSAURUS (arh-gen-TEEN-o-SORE-us) An extremely large member of the titanosaur family, this dinosaur may have been the biggest and heaviest of all, weighing up to 100 tons. Fossils have been found in South America. It lived 100 to 93 million years ago, during the Late Cretaceous period.

HYPACROSAURUS (hi-PACK-roe-sore-us) A genus of duck-billed dinosaur and a member of the lambeosaurine family. They grew to about 30 feet long and had almost 40 rows of tightly packed teeth, perfect for grinding tough plants. Fossils have been found in North America from the Late Cretaceous.

MAIASAURA (MY-a-SORE-a) This plant-eating dinosaur was a member of the hadrosaurine family and the first dinosaur species discovered to have nests with babies. They probably lived in large herds, traveling and grazing on plants. Fossils have been found in North America from the Late Cretaceous. Adults grew up to 26 feet long.

OVIRAPTOR (OH-vuh-RAP-tor) A small, bird-like theropod dinosaur. It was only 6 to 8 feet long, weighing about 60 pounds. It was lightly built and fast-moving, with 3-inch, curved claws on its hands. It had a toothless beak and powerful jaws. Fossils have been found in Asia in rocks from the Late Cretaceous.

PSITTACOSAURUS (SIH-ta-ko-sore-us) *Psittacosaurus* were small plant-eating dinosaurs that walked on two legs. They were an early member of the family of horned dinosaurs and ranged from 2.5 to 6 feet long. They had a parrot-like beak and some had hollow, tubular bristles arranged in a row down the tail. Fossils have been found in Asia from the Early Cretaceous.

TROODON (TRUE-o-don) A small, bird-like theropod, *Troodon* was a swift-running meat-eater with very large eyes, which might have helped it hunt at night. Adults were only 6 to 8 feet long. Its name, given for its jagged-edged teeth, means "wounding tooth." Fossils have been found in North America from the Late Cretaceous.

SALTASAURUS (SAHL-tah-SORE-us) Perhaps the largest armored dinosaur, this plant-eater had lumpy, boney plates on its back, which served as protection against meat-eating attackers. It was a medium-sized member of the titanosaur family, weighing as much as five elephants, and lived during the Late Cretaceous.

TYRANNOSAURUS REX (tie-RAN-oh-SORE-us-rex) The largest meat-eating dinosaur in North America. It was 40 feet long with 6-inch, dagger-like teeth. It is a member of the tyrannosaur family from the Late Cretaceous. Its name means "King Tyrant Lizard."

GLOSSARY

altricial: An animal species that is helpless at birth or hatching, and requires parental care for a period of time.

bonebed: A deposit of fossils that contains many bones, often from only one species of dinosaur.

brood: To sit on or hatch eggs.

burrow: A hole dug in the ground by an animal for shelter.

colony: A group of animals of the same species living closely together.

crèche: A grouping of young animals who are cared for communally.

crest: A hollow, bony ridge on a dinosaur's head.

embryo: A developing animal still inside an egg.

forage: To search for food.

fossil: The remains or traces of a once-living animal or plant preserved in rock.

hatchling: A young animal recently emerged from an egg.

herd: A large group of animals that travel and feed together.

incubate: To sit upon eggs to warm them.

mammal: Any of various warm-blooded vertebrate animals, characterized by hair covering the skin and, in the female, producing milk to nourish young.

paleontologist *(PAY-lee-un-Tol-oh-jist):* A scientist who studies fossils to learn about past life.

precocial: An animal species that is active and able to move freely from birth or hatching, and requires little parental care.

prey: An animal hunted for food by another animal.

predator: An animal that lives by hunting and eating other animals.

species: A distinct kind of plant or animal with certain common characteristics.

titanosaur: A diverse group of sauropod dinosaurs including *Saltasaurus* and *Argentinosaurus*. The group was widespread, ranging all over the world. All species of the family were plant-eating, four-legged dinosaurs with long necks and small heads.

trackway: A path or trail of fossilized footprints.

BIBLIOGRAPHY

Carpenter, Kenneth. *Eggs, Nests, and Baby Dinosaurs: A Look at Dinosaur Reproduction.* Bloomington: Indiana University Press, 1999.

Chiappe, Luis. *Glorified Dinosaurs: The Origin and Early Evolution of Birds.* New Jersey: John Wiley & Sons, Inc., 2007.

Chiappe, Luis and Lowell Dingus. *Walking on Eggs: The Astonishing Discovery of Thousands of Dinosaur Eggs in the Badlands of Patagonia.* New York: Scribner, 2001.

Currie, Philip J. "The Great Dinosaur Egg Hunt." *National Geographic* 189, no. 5 (1996): 96–109.

Currie, Philip J., Eva B. Keppelhus, Martin A. Shugas, and Joanna L. Wright. *Feathered Dragons: Studies on the Transition from Dinosaurs to Birds.* Bloomington: Indiana University Press, 2004.

Horner, Jack. *Dinosaurs: Under the Big Sky.* Missoula: Montana Press Publishing Company, 2001.

Meng, Qingjin, Jinyuan Liu, David J. Varricchio, Timothy Huang, and Chunling Gao. "Parental Care in an Ornithischian Dinosaur." *Nature* 431 (2004):145.

Sloan, Christopher. *Feathered Dinosaurs.* Washington, D.C.: National Geographic Society, 2000.

AUTHOR'S NOTE

As a child it wasn't hard for me to imagine how baby dinosaurs behaved. I was fortunate to have grandparents who were ornithologists (scientists who study birds) and I spent every summer helping them raise hawks and owls. I was interested in birds, but even more so with dinosaurs. When I turned 15, I wrote the Royal Tyrrell Museum of Paleontology in Alberta, Canada, and asked to volunteer on a dinosaur dig. Dr. Philip Currie, the curator of the museum, was kind enough to allow a teenager on his summer crew. I spent the next three summers digging up dinosaur bones, studying fossils, and expanding my imagination.

I graduated college with a degree in geology, but eventually realized that what I really loved was drawing and writing about dinosaurs. This book fulfills a lifelong dream to investigate paleontologists' understanding of baby dinosaurs and their parents. It was an exciting project because scientists have made many great new discoveries of fossilized baby dinosaurs, nests, and eggs in recent years.

Piecing together fossil clues is like detective work. Paleontologists still don't know exactly how baby dinosaurs behaved and looked. They follow a scientific method of gathering clues and reviewing evidence to make good guesses (called hypotheses) about dinosaurs. You can join in their detective work. Read the clues in this book to see how scientists think dinosaurs behaved. And because we now know birds evolved from dinosaurs, you can study the birds in your backyard. Make your own guesses about the behavior of baby dinosaurs. Never stop guessing. Someday *you* may have new ideas about what baby dinosaurs were really like.

ACKNOWLEDGMENTS

The author would like to thank Michael J. Ryan, Ph.D., Curator of Vertebrate Paleontology at Cleveland Museum of Natural History and Chief Paleontologist, Phaeton Group, for generously giving his time to review the manuscript for this book.

Published by Flash Point, an imprint of Roaring Brook Press.
Roaring Brook Press is a division of Holtzbrinck Publishing Holdings Limited Partnership
175 Fifth Avenue, New York, New York 10010
www.roaringbrookpress.com

Distributed in Canada by H. B. Fenn and Company Ltd.

Cataloging-in-Publication Data is on file at the Library of Congress
ISBN: 978-1-59643-443-1

Roaring Brook Press books are available for special promotions and premiums.
For details contact: Director of Special Markets, Holtzbrinck Publishers.

First Edition May 2010
Book design by Danica Novgorodoff
Printed in October 2009 in China by SNP Leefung Printers Ltd., Dongguan City, Guangdong Province.

1 2 3 4 5 6 7 8 9